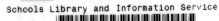

Looking at
Animals
in
HOT
PLACES

First published in Great Britain in 1999 by

 Belitha Press Limited,
London House, Great Eastern Wharf,
Parkgate Road, London SW11 4NQ

Copyright © Belitha Press Limited 1999
Text copyright © Moira Butterfield 1999

Series Editor Honor Head
Series Designer Hayley Cove
Picture Researcher Juliet Duff
Map Artwork Robin Carter / Wildlife Art Agency
Animal Symbols Arlene Adams

ISBN 1 84138 021 0

Printed in China

British Library Cataloguing in Publication Data
CIP data for this book is available from the British Library

Photographic credits
Frank Lane Picture Agency: 7,27,28 E & D. Hosking; 10 Panda/S.Vannini;
13,22 and 26 Gerard Lacz; 16 Leeson/Sunset; 18 Ron Austing;
19 Lewis W.Walker; 20 Chris Mattison; 29 Leonard Lee Rue.
NHPA: 21 Stephen Dalton. Planet Earth Pictures: 12 Alain Dragesco;17
Richard Coomber. Oxford Scientific Films: 6 Mickey Gibson; 8,15 Michael
Fogden; 9 London Scientific Films; 11 Konrad White; 14 Kathie Atkinson;
23 Root/Okapia; 24 Mike Linley; 25 J.A.L. Cooke.
Cover
Frank Lane Picture Agency: bottom Gerard Lacz.
Oxford Scientific Films: top.
London Scientific Films: centre right Mickey Gibson.

Looking at
Animals
in
HOT
PLACES

Moira Butterfield

Belitha Press

Introduction

There are many parts of the world where it is very hot. These hot places are called deserts, rainforests and grasslands.

Some deserts have hardly any rain and here there is nothing but sand. Other deserts are made of rocks and boulders. In some deserts it rains very hard once a year. Rainforests have a lot of rain and are very hot and steamy all year round. Grasslands are very dry for most of the time, but have lots of rain once a year.

Lots of animals live in these hot places, from tiny insects and strange looking lizards, to birds and big animals. They all have their own ways of living in the heat.

Contents

Camel

Camels live in deserts which are hot
and dry. They can go without food
and water for many days. Their feet are
big and wide which helps them to walk
on soft sand. In the deserts of Africa
people often use camels instead
of cars to carry them around.

Scorpion

Scorpions live in hot places, but they hide in the shade during the day. They come out at night when the weather gets cooler.

Scorpions eat insects and spiders.
They kill them with their strong claws.
They kill big insects with the sting
on the end of their tail.

Gorilla

Gorillas live in jungles which are hot and steamy. They eat lots of fruit and bark. They live in big family groups, headed by the strongest male. Adult gorillas can be three times as big as a grown man. Gorillas climb trees where they build a nest to sleep in.

Sand cat

The little sand cat lives in northern Africa.
It is wild, not tame and friendly like a
pet cat. It prowls around at night looking
for mice and snakes to eat.

It has sharp teeth and claws. The bottom
of its paws are hairy so it can walk on
hot sand without burning itself.

Moloch lizard

Lizards like hot places. This prickly moloch lizard lives in a desert in Australia. Sometimes it is called a thorny devil because its back is covered in sharp spines. The spines stop other animals attacking it. It has a long tongue that it uses to lick up ants from the ground.

Tapir

Tapirs live in swamps or near streams
in the jungle. They sleep in the daytime
and come out at night when it is cool.
They eat water plants and leaves.

They can swim well, which helps them
to escape bigger animals such as
jaguars who would like to eat them.

Elf owl

Birds live in hot places, too. This tiny elf owl is about the size of a coffee mug. It lives in America. It lays eggs in a hole in a tall, prickly cactus, where they will be safe from harm. The owl is too small to make its own hole so it looks for one that a bigger bird has made.

Rattlesnake

Snakes love warmth, so hot places are good homes for them. This rattlesnake lives in the American desert. It has sharp, poisonous fangs.

It has lots of tiny scales at the end of its tail. When it rattles them it is sending a message that means, 'Stay away!'

Hippopotamus

Hippos live in Africa. They spend the day keeping cool in the lakes and rivers. They leave the water at night to eat grasses and plants. Although they are very big and heavy, they are good swimmers. Hippos are very fierce and have huge teeth. They often fight each other.

Spadefoot toad

The American spadefoot toad has big feet for digging burrows in the desert. The toad hides underground for most of the year waiting for rain to come.

When the rain comes the toad hops out to lay its eggs in the rain puddles. The babies grow into adults in just two weeks.

Fennec fox

The fennec fox lives in African deserts.
It lives in a burrow in the sand. It has
big ears that help it to keep cool. When
the little fox gets too hot the heat from
inside its body passes out through its ears,
just like heat coming out of a radiator.
The fox's ears help it to hear well, too.

Tarantula

The red-kneed tarantula spider lives in deserts in Mexico. It hides in a burrow underground. It puts a few tiny silk threads outside the entrance to its burrow.

When a small animal walks by, the threads wobble. Then the tarantula jumps out and bites the animal with its poisonous fangs.

Where they live

This is a map of the world. It shows you where the animals live.

NORTH AMERICA
SOUTH AMERICA

- desert
- rainforest
- grassland

- camel
- scorpion
- gorilla
- sand cat
- moloch lizard
- tapir
- elf owl
- rattlesnake
- hippopotamus
- spadefoot toad
- fennec fox
- tarantula

EUROPE

ASIA

AFRICA

AUSTRALIA

Index of words to learn

bark the outside covering of a tree 11

burrow an underground home . . 25, 27, 29

cactus a plant with prickles, not leaves . . 19

claws sharp, pointed nails for scratching
or grabbing something 9, 13

fangs big, sharp teeth 21, 29

jaguar a big, fierce cat with a spotted coat . 17

jungle a forest in a hot place 11

scales tiny pieces of skin that overlap
each other 21

shade a cool, shadowy place 9

steamy hot and wet 4, 11

swamp a watery, muddy place 17

tame is friendly to humans 13